For Freya and Nat – G.A.

For Joel. Big love, always – A.B.

First published in 2002 by Macmillan Children's Books
a division of Macmillan Publishers Limited,
20 New Wharf Road, London N1 9RR,
Basingstoke and Oxford
Associated companies throughout the world
www.panmacmillan.com

ISBN 0 333 94910 2 HB
ISBN 0 333 94911 0 PB

Printed in Belgium by Proost.

Welcome to the World

by Giles Andreae

illustrated by Alison Bartlett

MACMILLAN CHILDREN'S BOOKS

Welcome from the flowers,

welcome from the trees,

welcome

from the butterflies,

welcome from the bees.

of every foreign land,

welcome from
the jungle,

welcome from the sand.

Welcome from the sunshine
and the birds up in the sky,

welcome from
the moon and from
the mountain-tops so high,

welcome from the ocean and the creatures of the sea,

and
welcome,
too, from
ME!